JOHN HAF

MW01202117

Stephanie's
STORY

It's Not
Your Time Yet
But Soon

outskirts
press

Dedication

First and foremost I dedicate this book to God my creator and His Son Jesus Christ, my savior. All honor and glory.

To my aunt and uncle, Larry and Ruth Ann Williams. To the Rev. Durwood Perry and his wonderful wife, Anne. To all the earthly angels that surrounded Belinda and me during this journey. To Nikki Watts; you stood by me. Love you, girl.

To my precious wife, Belinda, the special angel that God chose to walk through life with me.

To my grandson Johnathon and my granddaughters Belinda Grace (B.G.) and Barbara, you rock my world.

Last but not least to the memory of my daughter Stephanie, whose tragic death was the beginning of the journey. Without her life, death, and presence on earth, this book would not have been necessary or possible. See you on the other side, babe.

Table of Contents

Foreword

I CONSIDER IT a privilege to write this foreword in honor of Stephanie, John, Belinda, and their family. I met John and his family in 1990 when they attended the church where I was the "new" pastor at the time. Both our families' deep friendship began when Stephanie's accident happened. I have been a pastor for more than forty-seven years now and have done my best to comfort hundreds of families that have lost their loved ones and point them to the Great Comforter, the Holy Spirit for peace that only He can give. My wife, Anne, and I have been close friends with John, Belinda, and their family for thirty years. Also, my children went to school with and were friends with Stephanie.

When John asked me to write the foreword to *Stephanie's Story*, at first I was reluctant. I was reluctant not because of anything to do with the book or John, but because I had never written a foreword before, and I was afraid that I couldn't properly convey the significance of this story.

As their pastor and friend, I was with them during this time of heart-wrenching tragedy in their life. I felt inadequate to comfort and console them.

Their lives had been shattered into tiny pieces.

Mere words of "comfort" from even sympathetic lips seemed inadequate. All we could do was trust in God and the Holy Spirit to convey God's love through us by being there for them when they needed us.

Also I was fortunate to have a youth minister, Alan Folsom, his wife Paula, and youth workers who had built up a vibrant youth ministry group that had attracted Stephanie and other young people in the community to our church. As well as loving on John and Belinda during this tragedy they also played a significant role in why John and his family began attending our church.

I believe *Stephanie's Story* will help encourage those who read it to never give up on "putting the pieces back together" for life after a terrible tragedy. Whether it be the loss of a child, spouse, parent, or other significant loved one, or whether it be a divorce, or some other life-shattering event, never give up seeking God's peace and help to live again. You don't have to go through this journey alone.

Stephanie's Story will help those who struggle to keep their faith in God intact during the most devastating storms that come their way in life. John shares honest details about his personal wrestling with God for answers and meaning to the devastation of losing his beautiful, vibrant, thirteen-year-old daughter. It reminded me of the biblical story of Jacob wrestling with the angel of God and vowing not to let go until God gave him a blessing.

I would urge you, even if you've never experienced a terrible tragedy of this magnitude, to get *Stephanie's Story* and read it or pass it on to a friend who has experienced a tragedy in life.

I believe this story can help you in your life journey to know that there really is a God who has "broad shoulders" and can take your screaming questions or doubts. And if you are willing to honestly ask; seek; knock (not just once), but until you find Him; He will answer. He cares for you and is available to you.

Not only have John and Belinda been a blessing to our family, but their story has also enabled us to more effectively minister to others who have gone through similar tragedies in life.

My desire is, as is John's, that *Stephanie's Story* will inspire and be a blessing to your journey.

Durwood Perry, Pastor
Ball Ground, GA
2021

Preface

STEPHANIE'S STORY IS a book about life, death, and my personal struggle with the existence of a god, a journey from the light to the dark and back to the light. The story is true, not fabrication or fiction, and written not by an author or writer but by a dad wounded, heart-broken, and seeking to make order of a world without order.

My purpose for writing the book was not to win literary awards or recognition. The purpose is to provide hope and to let you know that as you travel through the dark valley you are not alone. It is a common book written by a common man in common terms for a common people. If you are reading this book you are just one, and there are many desperate dads, moms, siblings, and friends asking why and what now.

Several years after Stephanie's passing, my wife and I were sitting on our back porch. It was around eleven o'clock on a warm Georgia night, total silence except the sounds of chirping crickets. The silence was broken by the sound of screeching brakes and a loud bang, followed by a young girl screaming. We could hear the young girl crying out, "Oh my god, oh my god." Shortly thereafter the night air was filled with the sound of sirens.

The next day we learned that there were two young people returning home from their prom and the boy had backed out of the driveway into the path of an oncoming car.

He was pronounced dead at the scene. Two young people, their parents, grandparents, siblings, and friends, their lives altered forever, were cast into that dark valley. Another journey begins.

As I finished this book I received word that one of my grand-daughters' roommates at college was found deceased in her dorm room. She was a vibrant, intelligent young woman filled with much promise and much to give to the world. She had died from an allergic reaction to food she was eating. Another journey begins. My prayer is that no one will ever face the reality of losing a loved one, but we all know that is impossible.

One of the publishers I submitted my manuscript to gave an honest critique of the manuscript, saying that it lacked order.

I had to give some serious thought about that comment. They are the experts, right? They said it started out as an autobiography and then shifted to talking about others. I think that was a fair assessment. Indeed it does.

Without others the story would have had a much different ending. *"God has promised to be with us, to give His angels charge over us. Yet, by God's sovereign will and plan and for purposes of His own, He may allow disaster and suffering as He did with Joseph and Job and Peter and Paul."* (2 Kings 6:8-23)

God allowed the disaster and suffering and He gave His angels charge over me. The story cannot be told without them.

My life and probably yours, if you are on this journey, has no order. Life is like a puzzle scattered into a million pieces, with no rhyme or reason. We are just picking up the pieces and trying to fit them back into the box.

My hope and prayer is that through this book you can be encouraged to move forward in life knowing that you can survive.

The journey I have taken and the journey you are taking is painful. Nothing can take away the pain, and the pain is part of the process of healing. It is our pain, and it is okay for us to feel the pain. Feeling the pain is part of our recovery.

The five steps of grief are denial, anger, bargaining, depression, and acceptance. As we heal we go through these stages, not always in that order, and sometimes we are in multiple stages. Eventually we hope to arrive at the acceptance stage. Acceptance is letting go of that which we cannot control. As we let go of the darkness, the light will begin to shine and life will return.

Your pain, my pain, your grief and my grief, are ours and ours alone. Only we can feel what we feel, and only we can take the steps to complete our journey. There is no time frame for completion, and we must all journey at our own pace.

My hope is that through this book you will soon arrive at the destination you seek. Through perseverance and God's grace and mercy, your time for understanding, acceptance, peace, and happiness will return.

CHAPTER 1

In The Beginning

John and Belinda

IN THE BEGINNING God created the heavens and the earth. In the beginning God created John and Belinda, thus *Stephanie's Story*. Stephanie was the second child of a young couple, John and Belinda Hart, from southern West Virginia.

Belinda and I had known each other since an early age, dated in high school, and married shortly thereafter. Our first child was a son, followed by a daughter, Stephanie, seven years later. Belinda and I were both raised in middle-class families. My mother and father owned and operated a restaurant, and Belinda's father was employed in the mining industry. Her mother was a stay-at-home mom, busy raising four children and maintaining the homeplace.

Although we were from the traditional-type of family, we both lacked a father figure in our life. My father was a workaholic. With four children to support there was little time for father-son interaction. Belinda was raised on a small farm, and her father was a lot like mine. Both were involved with work and activities, and neither had time to attend activities that we were involved in.

In one sense she and I were complete opposites. She was the good girl, good student type, whereas I was a little more on the rebellious side. We certainly seemed a mismatch. I had known who she was from about the age of ten. Although we lived only four miles from each other, we attended different schools. We first became formally acquainted when I was sixteen and she was fifteen.

For me it was love at first sight. She filled a void in my life. She didn't always approve of my behavior, but she did understand me. My mother said that when I first met Belinda I came home and said, "I have met the girl I am going to marry," a bold statement for a sixteen-year old boy who had no idea where he was going in life or how he was going to get there. One thing I did know was that I wanted her to be a part of my future.

We dated on and off throughout high school, and after she graduated high school in 1969, we eloped. We had it all worked out.

Seeking employment, many of my family members had moved from West Virginia to the industrial belt in Ohio. I went to Ohio and found employment in a factory. I rented a furnished apartment in anticipation of the soon-to-be announcement to her parents that we were married.

Our plans were cut short when her mother found out what we had done. Her mother was irate. She threatened to have the marriage annulled and to have me jailed for taking Belinda across the state line, into Virginia, to be married. We had been married for several months, and Belinda informed her mother that she was pregnant, and regardless of how she felt, we were going to remain husband and wife. We selected a date, and I made arrangements for her to join me in Ohio.

We started with bare bones. No car, no furniture, no telephone. We had our clothes and a few items that we had received from family. One Friday evening after work, I rode a bus to West Virginia, and my sister drove the girl of my dreams and me back to Ohio. Monday morning it was just her and I, two micro specs in a vast world, surrounded by uncertainty about our future. Most people said, "It will never work." They gave it six months.

She was pregnant, and I was the only one working, making $1.65 an hour, which just didn't seem to go very far. From a very early age Belinda had helped prepare meals at her house, and her culinary skills really came in handy. Our diet consisted of biscuits, gravy, and fried potatoes. She could, and still can, take just a few staples and turn them into a pretty good meal.

I either walked to work, three miles each way, or occasionally caught a ride with another worker. I found a 1961 Chevrolet on a car lot, and the guy wanted $225 for it. I paid him $25 down and promised to pay $25 a week until the car was paid for. He was to keep the car until it was paid in full. I was working the eleven-to-seven shift, and every Friday morning I would wait until the bank was open, cash my check, and pay the $25. Eleven weeks later we had our first actual possession, an extremely used 1961 Chevy Biscayne.

We cleaned it and shined it and were as proud of it as if it were a new Mercedes. That's the way our relationship was and still is, always pulling together and working toward a common goal. She was, and is, the cream in my coffee. We were a perfect fit. She was the one who could take away my rough edges and inspire me to want more and be more.

After our son was born, Belinda joined the work force, and by the middle 1970s, we both had good careers. We were financially secure and able to enjoy many of the so- called fine things in life. In 1976

Stephanie was born, and I imagine in many ways, we would have been considered the ideal family.

Both children were good kids, good athletes, and did well in school. We were living life in the fast lane. We both were raised in semi-Christian families. You know the type? Church on Christmas and Easter, believed in the Father and Son, and tried to live a moral life. Our circle of friends included mostly professional people, and there was socializing and partying, nothing real serious, no drugs, but cookouts, dances, and a few drinks.

Life was wonderful. Each day was a new adventure. Brian was closer to his mother than he was to me. In retrospect I probably wasn't the best father, demanding and expecting perfection, and not giving enough praise when I should have. It seemed that the relationship between my son and me was strained from the beginning. I didn't know how to be a father. I was a reflection of my father, demanding and incapable of expressing love. I loved both of my children equally, though I doubt that I ever displayed it.

CHAPTER 2

The Warning

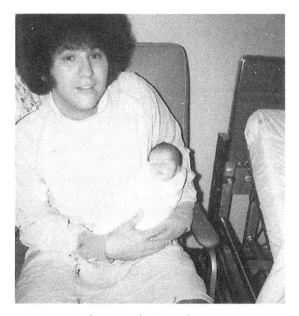

John and Stephanie

STEPHANIE WAS A daddy's girl, a delightful child, the apple of her daddy's eye. Where it seemed that I was almost always able to find fault in Brian, my relationship with Stephanie was just the opposite. She and I were very close, and an enormous bond developed between father and daughter.

Father and daughter, the world was theirs, at least until that fateful day, May 8, 1990.

Our family had moved to Georgia from Indiana in October 1987. I had accepted a position that provided increased financial security. We purchased a home in one of the nicer subdivisions in the county.

The job was demanding, and I was having to spend more time at my career.

Though we remained close, Stephanie was thirteen and growing into a young lady and preferred to spend more time with her friends, school activities, sports, etc. Brian had just graduated from high school and had made the choice to enlist in the military instead of attending college. From 1987 until 1990, it was just father, mother, and daughter at home.

Stephanie

In late 1989, I shared with Belinda that I was being burdened with the fact that we did not attend church regularly, and I was troubled with the thought that we needed to get Stephanie in church. I'm not sure where this feeling came from. It just seemed to come from nowhere, but it was something that I just couldn't shake.

We decided to visit different churches in the area. For the next several months we visited numerous churches until one Sunday morning I asked Stephanie where she would like to go to church that morning. She named a specific church, stating that a lot of her friends went there.

That was in November of 1989. We continued to attend the church on Sunday mornings. Somewhere around February 1990, during the invitation, a woman stood up (she was the pastor's wife, though I did not know it at the time) and stated that God had placed a burden upon her heart. "One of the children in the church is in grave danger." The woman was crying, and it was a very emotional scene.

It scared the hell out of me. I did not mention it again until several days later, and then I approached Belinda with the matter. I said, "What in the world is the matter with that woman? She must be a fruitcake to stand up and make such a statement!"

Her comment was really bothering me, and I shared the incident with a coworker. He said, "You know how religious people can be, getting caught up in the moment. I wouldn't give it much thought if I were you."

I could not shake it that easy. What was really eating at me was that I knew it was my child, the baby I had held at birth, the blue-eyed, black-haired beauty that had become the center of my life. I told Belinda that it would be a cold day in hell before I attended that church again.

Stephanie and her mother continued to attend church there, but I chose to stay home. I became more involved in my work, shutting the world out.

Even though I refused to go to church, God was already at work behind the scenes. The hardest time to see God's plans are when everything seems to have fallen apart. When we have been stripped of everything it can be difficult to remember that there is a loving God who has a plan. The Bible shows clearly that God sometimes allows terrible circumstances to move His plan forward.

Life continued as usual. It was late May, and school was just a few days from being out for the summer. Stephanie had been named to the all-A yearly honor roll, participated in basketball and soccer, and was looking forward to a summer of just kicking back and being with friends.

Sunday, May 6, 1990, I left for a three-day conference in Helen, Georgia. Stephanie walked me to the car, we hugged, and I started to back out of the driveway.

A strange feeling came over me. I stopped the car and just looked at her standing there in the driveway. Thirteen years flashed before my eyes.

I was scared and confused. I didn't want to go. Every ounce of energy in my body was telling me not to go, but I had to go.

She noticed that I was just staring at her, and when I shut off the car and stepped from it, she asked, the way teenagers do, "What?"

I replied, "Nothing, I just want you to know that I love you and that you are everything a father could desire in a daughter."

She smiled and replied, "Oh Dad, go to work."

It was a three-hour drive to Helen, and for me it seemed like an eternity. I was uneasy and agitated. When I arrived in Helen, the first thing I did after checking in was to call home. I asked Belinda, "Is everything okay?" She assured me that it was.

I talked to Stephanie and asked about her day. Before I hung up I said, "Baby, I love you, and I am so proud of you."

She laughed and said, "Dad, you're freaking me out."

At that point I realized that father and daughter had reached an awkward stage. She had grown beyond snuggling up on her dad's lap as we watched a scary show. It seemed as if to tell her that I loved her was embarrassing to her. I mean, after all, she was a teenager. Stuff like that was for kids.

The next day my time was consumed with the conference, and I was somewhat, but not totally, distracted from that nagging feeling. I agreed to meet some of my colleagues for dinner, but first chose to go to my room and shower. When I entered the room I noticed that the light on the telephone was flashing, indicating that there was a message. I called the front desk, and the clerk informed me that I was to call Belinda's work immediately.

Little did I know that my world was about to be shaken from its axis. My perfect world was about to be shattered, torn to pieces, and my heart ripped from my body.

If you are reading this you have probably experienced the same. Your perfect world changed in an instant.

I called her work, and one of her associates told me that Stephanie had been struck by a car and was being airlifted to the Columbus Medical Center. Belinda was in route with her. All I could do was ask, "Is my baby alive?"

All the associate could say was, "John, I don't know. You just need to get there as soon as possible."

I was an emotional wreck. A colleague, Roger Campbell, volunteered to drive me. Leaving everything behind, he drove as fast as he could to Columbus, Georgia, a four-hour trip. I could not stop crying or trembling. Roger kept reassuring me, trying to calm my fears. All I could say was, "Oh, please, God, please, let my baby be alive."

CHAPTER 3

The Light Turns to Darkness

WHEN I ARRIVED at the Medical Center I was directed to the emergency room. My wife, family, friends, and many of Stephanie's classmates were crowded into the waiting room and hallway.

I saw my wife, the woman who had been my constant companion and friend for more than twenty-five years. Her eyes were hollow. The radiant beauty that has always shown from her face was a pale gray, empty, and lifeless. My first question was, "Is my baby alive?"

She told me that she was unconscious from the moment that she was struck and that the doctors were with her. We sat and waited, and about an hour later, the hospital staff moved her to a special unit on the fourth floor.

When they wheeled her bed out of the emergency room and I saw her, my knees buckled. Her body was swollen, her eyes blackened, and her head bandaged. She looked nothing like the young girl standing in the driveway.

"Oh baby, oh baby," was all I could say.

The doctors told us that she had suffered serious head trauma, but at that time they could not, or would not, give us a prognosis of her future condition.

They placed her in a special unit for twenty-four-hour care. It was about midnight, and everyone had left. It was just Belinda and me. We sat by her bed, each holding a hand, talking to her.

I told her, "It is going to be all right. Daddy is a fixer. He is always able to make things right. I'll fix it!" I told the doctors to spare no expense. It did not matter if they had to fly doctors in or transport her to another facility; I wanted the best. I would make it right again.

They mostly just looked at me sympathetically and said, "We are doing all that we can, Mr. Hart." They knew from the beginning that any effort would be wasted effort.

By morning family members from out of state had started to arrive. The hallways were filled with her friends and classmates. People were bringing food.

Her condition remained the same. unresponsive.

All through the day, nurses and doctors passed by and people stood in small groups, talking about various subjects. I wanted to stand up and scream out, "God, people, what's wrong with you? My baby is clinging to life, and you are talking about topics that are of absolutely no importance."

In the evening everyone would empty out, and it would be just Belinda, Stephanie, and me. On the morning of the third day, the doctor told us that he was going to do a test to measure the activity of her brain waves. Later that same day he came back and told us that there was no brain activity and that Georgia law required that they wait twenty-four hours and test again before he could legally pronounce a person deceased. "Bullshit," I said. "Your machine is screwed up. My baby is not dead!"

I guess inside I knew what the outcome was going to be, but damn it, I fix things. If the doctors couldn't fix it I'd take it to a higher authority. Then it dawned on me that I didn't personally know a higher authority.

CHAPTER 4

Let's Make A Deal

THE FIRST PERSON I had called after the accident was my aunt Ruth. She had always been more like a sister than an aunt, and if anyone had a connection to the higher authority, it was her. Of all the Christians I have known or will ever know, I can't imagine anyone having a greater faith than her. She assured me that she and all her friends were praying. I took my wife by the hand, asked the nurse if there was a chapel in the hospital, and proceeded to the chapel.

Understand this: In twenty-five years, my wife and I had never gotten down on our knees together and prayed. Truth is, I had never gotten down on my knees and prayed at all. What was the need? I believed in God and went to church occasionally. Wasn't that enough? Heck, I didn't even know how to pray a real prayer. You know what I mean? What I did was try to strike a business deal.

I said, "God, you know what this girl means to me. I give you my word, if you will let her survive, I'll live a better life and go to church more often." It was the sort of prayer that left me feeling that we should shake hands on it; after all, that's what you do when you finalize a deal. There. That should take care of it. Things will be better tomorrow. Ruth Ann and all her friends are praying, and we had prayed.

The next morning the test was repeated with the same result. No brain activity. Doctors and family members wanted to know what we were going to do. They said that she was dead and that they needed permission to remove her from life support.

Do what? You want me to give you permission to pull the plug on my world? What kind of beasts are you people? That's my baby. I asked that the test be run again and that Belinda and I wanted to be present.

The nurses took little patches and placed them on her scalp and head. They said that if they pinched her or pricked her with a needle, if there was brain activity, it would register on the graph. I took my baby's hand and talked to her. I said "Baby, this is Dad, you have to hear me, baby. You have to give these people a sign that you hear me." I started telling her funny stories about things we had experienced in the past.

"Remember the time we turned the canoe over? What about the time I threw the big rock and it got caught in a tree and came roaring back at me? Remember, baby? Please remember, baby."

When I looked up I could see the pain in the doctors' faces. I wonder how many times they had watched the same scenario unfold.

It was the fourth day. I had run out of options. Dr. Shannon came in and sat with my wife and me. I could see the pain and hurt on his face. I'll never forget his words. He said, "I went home last night. I have a daughter who is the same age as Stephanie. I looked down at her as she lay sleeping. I thought about what she means to me, how my life would change without her presence. I don't know what you folks are experiencing, and I'd not pretend to. What I do know is that Stephanie has passed on. She cannot and will not come back. As hard as the decision is to make, I know that there is no decision. She is no longer with us. As much as I love my daughter, my medical experience tells me that the end is final. I'll pray for you and your family as you choose your next step, but if my daughter were lying there, hooked up to all those machines, a lifeless body, I would have to let her go."

My wife and I returned home for the first time in four days. Our house was full of family members, and the activity was more than I could take. I went for a walk down into the woods. I wrapped my arms around a tree and cried out in pain. "Somebody help me! Please, somebody help me!"

It was just about dark when I came out of the woods. My decision was made. I mean, after all, that's what I do; I make decisions. I first spoke with my wife, and we agreed, and then I told all those present that we were going to remove Stephanie from life support. If any of them wanted to spend some time with her beforehand that they should. In the morning we would go to the hospital, have our private time with her, and leave.

CHAPTER 5

The Journey Begins

AT 11:00 A.M. on the fifth day, when we arrived at the hospital a doctor and a representative from a group called Lifeline of Georgia approached us and asked to speak to us. We went into a room. I asked Ruth to go with us, and they asked us if we would consider donating Stephanie's organs. Wow! First they ask us to take her off of life support, and now they want to know if we will give parts of her away. I asked my aunt if doing that was acceptable to God. Would we be breaking some commandment or violating some biblical teaching?

She said that it was okay, and if anyone knew if it was okay, Ruth knew. We agreed to donate her liver and kidneys, but I couldn't give up her heart. Strange, isn't it? She had the heart of an athlete, a strong heart that would offer life to another person, but I could not donate her heart.

After we signed the papers required for donation, we went into her room and had our final moments with her. I held her hand and could feel the warmth and feel her heart beat. I looked at the hands that had shot a basketball, thrown a softball, combed her long black hair, and thrown snowballs at her dad.

I told her, "I'm sorry, baby, Daddy can't fix it." Her eyes were black and her face swollen from the trauma. I leaned over and kissed her gently on the forehead and slowly let her fingers slip from my grasp, letting go of my world, and we turned and left.

It was Memorial Day weekend, so we waited until Tuesday to have her service. Family visitation was Monday evening, and I requested that the family remain behind at the house for an hour or so, so that my wife and I could visit her in private.

The previous day we had made the arrangements, selected the casket, etc. I'll never forget the attendant explaining all the different makes and models of caskets. Steel or wood? Cement or steel vault? What color? I thought, Hell, it's like buying a car. My mind was racing. Fog surrounded me, and my fog lights weren't burning. I asked the guy, "Which one is the best?" He went into spiel about a particular model, the features, etc. I shut him off, told him, "Spare me the details; we'll take it." As hard as the arrangements were, nothing could have prepared me for the next day.

As morning dawned I could tell it was going to be one of those hot, humid Georgia days. I remember thinking, "Damn humidity. No, damn world."

My wife and I dressed and went to the mortuary. As we exited the car and walked across the parking lot, I could see the heat reflecting off the asphalt. Damn heat. No, damn world.

We were met at the door by an attendant who escorted us to the chapel. He stopped at the entrance, and after we entered, he shut the doors behind us. I looked down the aisle, maybe fifty feet, and the realization of just how final it was hit me like a freight train.

My chest tightened. I couldn't breathe. My body was soaked with my own sweat. My wife and I clung to and supported each other, holding each other up as our world slipped away. Could we walk that fifty-foot distance? It seemed like a mile. As we started the journey to our daughter's side, it was as if we were walking in a tunnel, and the closer we got, the narrower the tunnel became, suffocating me, bearing down upon me, crushing my body. And with each of my steps, her body, lying there in the casket, became clearer and more vivid. When we reached the casket, I collapsed to my knees, and all I could do was cry out, "Oh, my god! Oh, my god! My baby! My baby. Damn you, God. Damn you. world."

I touched her hand. It was cold. She was dead. She looked dead. Whatever it is that beams out from people, their personality, persona, or whatever you might call it, is no longer there when you are dead. There's nothing but a lifeless body.

After a while family members arrived, and a short time later, the place was overflowing. Flowers lined every wall and spilled over into the aisle. The attendants asked me if they could take some of them to the nursing homes to make space. I told him it was okay with me. Damn the flowers. Damn the nursing home. Damn the world!

People came up to me, shaking my hand and telling me how sorry they were and how much they were hurting. I thought, hurt, hell! That's not your daughter lying there in a casket. Don't talk to me about your hurt. One man said, "God has picked another flower for his flower garden."

Do what? I'm not concerned with any damn flower garden or for that matter any damn god. Get that nonsense away from me. Where was God when I needed him?

The woman who was driving the car that struck Stephanie showed up at the visitation. I now understand that she meant well, but the timing was not good. She approached Belinda, expressing her sorrow, and a close friend, George Garten, kindly escorted her away. I just give thanks to God that it wasn't me she approached. I'm sure it would not have gone well with her.

The next morning started as the previous one, hot and humid. The service was scheduled for eleven o'clock. My house was full of people, family members who had traveled from other states and friends who had stopped in. In one way the atmosphere was much like a circus, minus the clowns and trapeze artists.

As my wife and I were getting dressed, everything was matter-of-fact. Neither of us had much to say. I guess we knew that the time was rapidly approaching for the final goodbye. When I look back on it, it seems strange, but as long as the deceased person's body is present, it really doesn't seem final. Although spiritually she was no longer present, we still had a physical remnant to cling to.

We arrived at the chapel a little before eleven, and as is customary, the family members were taken to a side room until the other attendees were seated. There was an eerie silence in the room. We all basically sat or stood as if we were shrouded in death. I guess we were. The attendant came and led the family into the chapel. As we walked down the center aisle I could see her classmates and friends seated to the left and others were seated to the right. My sight and thoughts were fixed on her classmates and friends.

These were the kids who had participated with her in sports and school activities, pajama parties, birthday parties, skating events that she would no longer be a part of. Millions of kids in the world and hundreds were sitting in the chapel. Why not one of them? Why my daughter?

The service was a blur. The minister, Reverend Durwood Perry, officiated. I had come to know him slightly through the church that Stephanie and Belinda attended. His son and daughter were classmates of Stephanie's.

There she lay, no more than ten feet away. As hymns were sung and words spoken, they were nothing more to me than a leaf fluttering in the wind. Was I to get comfort from the singing or the sermon? Were music and words somehow miraculously going to strengthen or encourage me? The time for miracles had passed. Now let the dead bury the dead. There was no more life in me than there was in her. The only difference was that she was at rest. I was in pain.

At the conclusion of the service, the cars, led by a police escort, wound through the city streets to the cemetery, her final resting place. The end of the journey.

Months before the accident, Stephanie and I had been at the cemetery visiting the grave of a friend of mine. She had commented on how close together the people were buried. I said to her, "That's all the room you get, baby; that's all the room you need."

She said, "I don't want strangers buried beside me when I die."

At the time, her comment had no impact, but when we selected her final resting place, the conversation came back to me. I selected eight plots. To the right and the top were walkways, and I purchased four plots below. I had honored her request. No stranger could be buried beside her.

My wife and I sat in the car as others parked and gathered at the gravesite, and then the attendant led us to the tent that covered her grave and sat us in front. The temperature was well into the nineties and the humidity was unbearable. Damn the heat; damn the humidity. Damn the miracle maker!

I have no recollection of the service. My attention was fixed on the casket. It was white, trimmed in gold, and inside it was my treasure.

The graveside service ended, and I wrapped my arm around my wife, my daughter's mother, and supported her back to the car.

We arrived back home only to be surrounded by family members and friends. It had been seven days since this painful journey had begun. It was time for everyone to leave, go home, and let me die a quiet death. Someone told me several years later that I had asked everyone to leave, that we wanted to be alone. I don't remember that.

CHAPTER 7

Reaping in the Fields

THERE WERE A lot of things that I didn't recall. Maybe as a defensive measure my brain had shut down. Maybe there were things I didn't want to remember. Maybe a person who is carrying the weight of the world on their shoulders, a person whose heart has been ripped from his very being, a person who has had the very breath of life sucked from him as a sponge sucks up liquid or as a vacuum sucks up dust is incapable of memory.

As family and friends started leaving to return home, someone remarked that we could begin our recovery. Begin our recovery? Hell, we're not alcoholics or drug addicts. We haven't broken a leg or sprained our back. We had parted with the gift that God had given us and that God had taken away. Oh, this is good. Someone left a card. How nice!

There is never a life without sadness,
There is never a heart free of pain;
If one seeks in this world for true solace,
He seeks it forever in vain.
So when to your heart comes the sorrow,
Of losing some dear one you've known;
'Tis the touch of God's sickle at harvest,
Since he reaps in the fields he has sown.

Well, isn't that sweet? This god plants a seed that grows into a beautiful teenager and then he just gets his ol' sickle and starts harvesting his crop.

I found no comfort in thinking that God just plants his little seeds, and when he felt the need for more flowers in his flower garden, he just grabs up his sickle and chops away.

I heard a preacher say that God was love. Do what? Say what? Love? Well, preacher, maybe you can explain to me how this loving God of yours decides which flower he is going to harvest. Does he flip a coin? Is there a lottery? I had never met a preacher or theologian who could answer that question. Oh, but they could say, "There are many mysteries of God that we cannot understand. But someday all will be revealed."

I had a message for the preacher. Something was being revealed. He was as phony and full of crap as the supposed god that he worshiped and served.

What a crock!

Questions Without Answers

A WEEK LATER my wife and I both returned to work. Our son had returned to the military, family members had returned home, and Stephanie's friends had started their summer break. It was just my wife and I, and there was a problem. We were a chain with a missing link. One of the links of the chain was missing, and we were no longer connected. We couldn't pull together. We were divided and separated. We couldn't even talk about what had happened.

The first thing I needed to know was how did it happen? We went to the state police headquarters and got the police report. The answer wasn't there. Sure, there were measurements, sketches, and a short summary. From the report I could see what had happened, but I wanted to know how it had happened.

How had someone intruded into the sphere of protection I provided my daughter, influenced her to get onto a dirt bike, which in due course led to her losing control of the bike and darting into oncoming traffic?

I discovered that the day before the accident (Monday), several teenagers from another subdivision in our area had come through our neighborhood on dirt bikes. They were acquaintances of Stephanie's from school. She was in the driveway playing basketball and the boys pulled into the driveway to talk to her.

Belinda told the boys that it was illegal to ride the dirt bikes on public roads and they should not bring them back onto our property. She also informed Stephanie that she was not to ride the dirt bikes.

The next evening (Tuesday) after school, and before Belinda arrived home, one boy returned. Again, Stephanie was in the driveway shooting baskets, the boy pulled into the driveway, and they talked. He was going to teach her how to ride the dirt bike. Whether it was his suggestion or hers, we will never know.

She got on the bike, with him behind her, and they rode to the mouth of the subdivision, where our street connects to the main road. He stated that as she went to make a U-turn to go back into the subdivision, she lost control, the bike accelerated, flipping him off the back, and shot out into traffic, where she and the bike were struck by an approaching automobile.

It was now three weeks after the accident, and I not only knew how, I also knew who. I had identified the one who was responsible. My pain and suffering were being masked beneath the anger and rage. The fuse was slowly burning.

Someone had suggested that we should seek grief counseling. I have no idea who made the suggestion, who made the appointment, and have no recollection of the first session. What I do know is that Belinda told me later that after the first session, the therapist had told her to keep a close eye on me. She had a perception of an angry outburst coming. The fuse was slowly burning.

Four weeks had passed. I now knew how it had happened, why it had happened, and the people responsible for it happening, the boy on the dirt bike and the woman driving the car. The pain was unbearable, the anger uncontrollable, and a reason for living nonexistent. Burning, slowly burning.

Each evening revolved around a trip to the cemetery, making sure the flowers were arranged perfectly, that no leaves or trash had found rest on her spot; my spot. My memorial was the one place where I could talk to her, knowing that all that separated us was several feet of earth.

The volcano searing inside of me was starting to spew hot ash and fire. It was visible to others that the eruption was near.

I had to fix it. I sat at her grave and made a promise to her that Dad would make it right. Somehow I had to have control. It was my responsibility; always had been, always would be.

Saturday morning I decided to go into work for a little while. I was a salaried employee and not required to work on Saturdays. The plant manager called me into the Resource office and started rambling about how I was not the same person and that I needed to be more focused on my job.

The slow-burning fuse accelerated, and the explosion erupted. "Listen, asshole, how in the hell do you know what I need to do? You have no idea what I am going through, and I couldn't care less about what you think." I got up slammed the door, stormed out of work, went home, got two pistols, and drove to the cemetery. I sat by my daughter's grave and told her that I would soon be with her, but first there was some unsettled business I needed to tend to. I was going to kill the boy and the woman and then kill myself. The score would be settled and I would finally be free. I sat there, my hands shaking as I held the guns. The damn heat; always the damn heat.

A coworker called my wife and told her that I had stormed out. She in turn called the therapist and our family doctor. My wife knew deep inside what I was going to do. She has known me since we were teenagers, and she knew where I was headed and what my intentions were.

For some reason, I don't know why, I returned to the house. I don't know why. I do know that there was a nagging feeling, a small voice saying, "Dad don't do it, please don't do it." I didn't know anything. There was no rhyme or reason to anything anymore. The world was spinning out of control, and I was just along for the ride. I returned home.

My wife was just leaving to house to come to the cemetery. She confronted me, and I told her my intentions.

"You can't, John! That's not what Stephanie would want." She pleaded with me and told me that she had talked to the therapist and our doctor and that they were going to help me. "Please try it before you do this."

She gave me a glass of water and a pill that the doctor had given her to give to me. I went out like a light. Five weeks of sleepless nights, the emotion, the stress, had overcome me. When I came to, I was in a hospital. Not just any hospital, a psychiatric hospital. Damn! They had committed me to a full-blown nut house.

Damn the nut house. Damn the doctor. Damn the world. Damn the god that harvested from the field he had sown. I wasn't crazy. I was mad as hell and bent on revenge.

Off To The Loony Bin

SEEING THAT I was not going to cooperate with the plan, the doctors knocked me out again. I awoke the next morning to see a young woman standing in my doorway. She was dressed in a hospital gown. She didn't say a word, she just stood there and urinated. A puddle formed at her feet. Jesus Christ! What am I doing in this place? Wait! There can't be a Jesus Christ. Was he not the supposed son of God? Don't tell me that this same god that harvested my daughter had stood silently by and watched his son be harvested. Get real. No father would or could do that.

"I'm not staying; that's the bottom line. It's not negotiable."

My wife said she was the only one who could check me out , and the only way she would do it was if I agreed to go to a private hospital in Columbus, Georgia, a real nice place. Not a state hospital like the one I was in, but a place with a dining hall and a pool. Bullshit! Putting in a dining hall and a pool doesn't change the fact that it is a nut house. Damn it! I'm not crazy. I'm mad as hell and bent on revenge, and they might delay justice, but justice would be served.

"Okay, I'll play along. I'll go to the fancy nuthouse. I have the answers they want to hear. In two weeks they'll see that there is nothing wrong with me, and I'll be released. Yeah, I'm street wise. I'll play their game. But they'll lose."

By that afternoon I was in the Bradley Center in Columbus. Let the games begin. The center was like a fancy hotel. Private rooms, a large lobby to relax in, and three meals a day with white linen and real silverware.

A person couldn't ask for a better field on which to play the game. There were about twenty people there. It was a private facility, quite expensive, and if your insurance didn't cover it, you had to pay the bill yourself. Yeah, a real nice place. A damn nut house, but a real nice nut house.

I sat in the lobby watching television, There were magazines and books everywhere. I went from table to table checking out the reading material. Oh my, look what we have here: a bible. Isn't that nice? Let me see, I can read the book written by the god who harvested my daughter and find comfort? Isn't that amazing? I picked up the book. So this is where the answers are? That's what my dear Christian friends keep telling me. "You will find comfort in God's word." I'll play along. Before I am finished, I'll know this book better than anyone. The next time bible thumpers spout scripture to me, I will be very well prepared to counter their foolishness.

The next morning the first stop was to meet with a counselor, Dr. Edwin Chase. Not only was he a psychiatrist, he was also an ordained Methodist minister. Now this should be interesting. Isn't this how it works? God harvested from his field and, now he sends in reinforcements to tell me how much he loves me and how someday I'll see more clearly and understand. Little did they know that my vision is perfect and I have great comprehension. It's easy to see and understand that Dr. Chase is full of shit, the world is full of shit, and those who cling to this "loving God" are full of shit.

Dr. Chase was a nice enough fellow, small in stature, middle aged, soft spoken. He wanted me to take a test. All right! Two thousand dollars a day, and they want me to take a test. I'm game. What fools these people are. Throw a little mumbo jumbo psyche crap on me, and abracadabra, all is well. Let the testing begin. I know the answers.

I obliged him by taking his test. He said that we would be meeting daily in an individual session and that there would also be a daily group session. Hot dog! A room full of nut jobs all gathered together. Now that should be fun.

I carried that bible with me at all times. During one of my daily meetings with Dr. Chase he asked me why I carried it. Here we go.

"Well, Dr. Chase," I replied, "I guess the correct answer is that I find comfort in God's word. That God is my strength, my refuge. But the truth is that this book is a fairytale, a book written by weak-minded people for weak-minded people. People who can't face or handle reality, so they embrace a mysterious father who provides for their needs here on earth and even into some mysterious utopia for all eternity. Oh yes, I read this book, I study this book, not to give glory or honor to some nonexistent heavenly father, but to expose it for what it is. Total nonsense.

After lunch all the residents, as we were called, gathered in the main room for free time. Read a book, watch television, play cards or a board game, or just sit around and chat. It was during this time that the assistants mingle with the nut jobs. It didn't take a genius to figure out that their responsibility was to glean information from the residents and report back to the head nut doctor, sort of like the song, "Just dropped in to see what condition my condition was in." Yeah, yeah, oh yeah, this will be fun.

One of the attendants, a nice-looking middle-aged woman, approached me. "Good Morning, Mr. Hart. How are you this morning?"

"Well, ma'am, I'm just as fine as the fuzz on a freshly picked peach." I thought, what a stupid question. Hell, lady, I'm angry, pissed off at the world, bent on revenge, and you want to know how I am this morning? Ask the doctor, ask my friends, ask the world; they'll tell you. I'm in a nut house. Surely I must be nuts.

I had to remind myself, remember the game, John, remember the game.

She sat, and we chatted. She was a nice woman, probably someone's mother or grandmother. She looked the part.

I played it perfectly, like a tennis game at Wimbledon. She would serve, and I would return volley. After a while she moved on to converse with some other nut job.

"Group time, group time," an assistant called out. Time to gather up all the loose screws, toss them into the same bag, and see how many emerge with their nut attached to their screw. Isn't that the way it works? You start with a loose screw and continue to tighten the nut until everything is secure.

Into the room we went, a bare room with just chairs in a circle. Sitting in the center of the circle was another nut doctor. This guy had the personality of a cinder block. After we were all positioned in the circle, about ten altogether, the good doctor announced that the group was being joined by a new resident. Why didn't he just say, "Another nut has fallen off the tree, and we are going to attach all you nuts back to the branches from which you have fallen"? He had each of us introduce ourself and state what our reason for being there was.

"My name is Mary. My husband is an alcoholic. His drinking is destroying our marriage, and I just can't cope with it anymore."

Shit, that shouldn't be too hard to fix. Toss his ass out and find you another man.

"My name is Gary. My wife left me, and I was abused as a child. I just can't seem to move forward."

You have be kidding me. Kick your dad's ass, and then get out and find you another woman. Try Mary there; she's needing a new man.

"My name is Marcus. I am addicted to cocaine."

Well hell, Marcus, am I supposed to feel sorry for you? You're the one who made the decision to suck powder up your nose. They oughta lock your ass up on a deserted island for ten years, or at least until you grow up and learn to accept responsibility for your actions.

And then there was Francis. She was a registered nurse, an attractive woman, well educated, classy, and with a quiet demeanor. Francis was the craziest one out of the whole damn bunch. She said she came to the center for two weeks each year just to collect herself.

Do what? You check yourself into the nut house just so you can sit around in a circle and tell people how bad you feel or how the world has dumped on you? Yep, this one is absolutely crazy.

The good doctor then turned to me. "John, would you like to introduce yourself?"

"No, not really, but if it pleases this distinguished group gathered here, my name is John, and there ain't a thing wrong with me."

The doctor just stared at me and I at him. Damn the doctor. Damn the group. Damn the world. Two more weeks of the same daily routine followed. Each day members of the group shared their stories. Each day it became more boring. What a bunch of whiners!

Gary, the guy whose wife had left him and was abused as a child, was about thirty years old. He was hearing impaired and wore a hearing aid. It seems that there was a short in the hearing aid and it would regularly start shrilling and shoot sound waves into his ear. When it happened, he banged on the side of his head.

Same thing, day after day. I was always the last one the good doctor would ask. "John, is there anything you would like to share with the group today?"

Same answer, day after day. Not a thing!

One day, after an extremely long session and watching Gary bang the side of his head numerous times, the good doctor asked, "John, is there anything you would like to share with the group today?"

I replied, "Why doesn't someone get that boy's hearing aid fixed before he beats his brains out with his own hand?"

The next day his hearing aid was repaired. After the session he came to me and thanked me. He said that I was the first one who had cared. I thought to myself, cared? Hell, I was just tired of seeing you beat the side of your head. As far as you hearing what is being said, trust me, you aren't missing a thing.

He thought I cared? He thought I had compassion for him? Compassion and caring was not within my inner being. I was a wounded bear hell bent on revenge and apparently a genuine certified nut job. Maybe they will give me a diploma when I graduate.

"This certificate is presented to John Hart in recognition that he is nuts but yet through counseling with medically trained normal people he has overcame his desire to kill people and can now be safely returned to society." If they believe that, then I know who the nut jobs are.

Third week first day, here we go again. "John, do you have anything you would like to share with the group?" "No, sir, not a thing." The doctor fixed his eyes on mine and stared. "My friend," he said, "you have anger inside of you."

I replied, "First of all, you are not my friend. Secondly, unless you have buried your child, you have no idea what is inside of me. Dumb ass. You can't learn that in medical school."

This thing was going nowhere. Impatience was starting to set in. This was a waste of time. I had more important things to do.

CHAPTER 9

Game Over

THERE WERE HAPPENINGS behind the scene that I was not aware of. The doctors were busy instituting a plan to break through the hard exterior barrier I had surrounded myself with.

I had grown closer to the group and would share some things with them. They knew the circumstances that had brought me to the Bradley Center and in some strange way they seemed more preoccupied with my well-being than their own. After dinner we would go for a walk through the park or sit by the pool and talk. Maybe they were making progress with their issues, and possibly what I was feeling from them was sympathy and concern because of my lack of progress. Either way, it didn't matter. It wasn't progress that I sought. It was revenge and relief.

One night we said our good nights and headed to our rooms. I opened the door, turned on the light, and came face to face with reality.

Lying on the bed was my daughter's basketball jersey, neatly folded with the number twenty-one glaring right at me like the light on a train roaring through a dark tunnel. I stood frozen, unable to move. Visions and flashbacks. I could see her taking a jump shot or leading a fast break, her hair in pigtails as she flashed me a smile.

My baby! Oh God, my baby!

I collapsed beside the bed crying uncontrollably. I took her jersey in my hands and clutched it to my chest. I could feel her, smell her, sense her presence. Help me, please help me. Oh baby, I love you. Please help me. I can't go on.

The barrier was down. I was nothing more than a broken man with a broken heart. Something had left my body, and there was no fight left in me.

A week later I was discharged from the Bradley Center. I continued to receive grief counseling several times a week. Sometimes it was individual counseling, and sometimes my wife and I received joint counseling.

It had been six weeks since Stephanie's accident, and during that time my total attention had been focused on anger, revenge, and me. I had been totally oblivious to the pain and suffering Belinda, the most important person in my life, was enduring. Together we tried to rebuild our shattered lives. One step forward and two steps back.

One evening we were sitting in our family room and I asked her, "Are we going to make it?"

"I don't know," she replied.

We wept.

We had been constant companions since the age of seventeen. We were husband and wife, best friends, soul mates, and mother and father. Our life had revolved around our children, and we were faced with the enormous task of rebuilding the chain with one link missing. We were not pulling together, strengthening each other. We were drifting apart like two shipwreck survivors being tossed about by waves of grief and torment.

I had read somewhere that when couples lose a child, 12 percent of the marriages end in divorce. Would we become another statistic, or would we beat the odds? If our relationship were to survive it would take someone or something stronger than I was. Lately every time I rolled the dice, they kept coming up snake eyes.

Though I was still full of anger, it was a controllable anger. Making use of therapy, family, friends, and Stephanie's friends, we started the long process of recovery. I guess we were addicts after all. We were addicted to being a strong family unit, addicted to the pleasure of watching our children grow, socializing with other parents at events and functions, and addicted to being mom and dad.

When someone dies family, friends and neighbors visit and gather to offer their condolences. Filled with good intentions, they offer their advice. One person said we would have to do away with Stephanie's room. She wasn't buried yet, and the solution was to do away with her room? Shovel the dirt on her casket, shovel the dirt on her life, that's the solution? Pretend it never happened, that she never existed? Bury my thoughts, feelings, and emotions?

These people meant well, but I didn't need someone to talk to me. I needed someone to listen to me. Wrap your arms around me, love me, listen to me. Cry with me, rejoice with me as I remember.

Never, never tell someone you know how they feel. We don't want to hear about what you experienced, how you dealt with it, and surely not what we need to do. When we are talking we are not looking for a response; we just want to be heard. We seek an ear, not a solution.

CHAPTER 10

Earthly Angels, Joy, Joy, Joy

AFTER I WAS released from the Bradley Center, my uncle and aunt, Larry and Ruth Ann Williams, and their daughter Lisa traveled every weekend from their home in Tennessee to our home in Georgia, a round trip journey of about five hundred miles.

My uncle and I had worked in the same industry, and as adults, Belinda and I had lived in the same towns they had. We had become in one sense closer to them than we were with our brothers and sisters.

When I had received the news of Stephanie's accident, the first person I called was Ruth Ann. She was more like an older sister than an aunt. I had spent my early childhood years with my grandmother, and Ruth Ann had lived briefly with my mom and dad when she was in high school. I don't think I have ever known a person with such strong faith in God. It seemed a little poignant that in my time of need I had sought out the person I believed to have the strongest faith, yet in my time of need, the one in whom she placed her faith failed to deliver on his promises.

Why was she coming? Did she know something that I didn't? To her credit, she didn't bible thump me. Was she there to see that I went to church each Sunday? That's where she had me.

Church wasn't all that bad. Most of the people were actually quite nice and pleasant to be around. We had also became close to the minister and his wife , Durwood and Ann Perry. Their children, Jeremy, Julie, and Jason provided temporary relief to our two broken hearts.

The first thing I knew, I had gotten saved. That's right, my name was on the church roll. I had been baptized, and I was volunteering for more work at the church than three men could handle. Yes sir, I was a born-again Christian.

Did that make me feel better? Was my heart mended? Had the sun broken through the clouds and once again was shining brightly before my path? Nope! Not in the least.

I discovered that a good number of the sisters and brothers were at least, if not more, miserable than I was. Where was all this joy, joy, joy, down in your heart? It wasn't in believing that God created the earth, that Jesus was the son and died for my sins, in being baptized, or being a member of the church.

I had been at this for about six months. I was a toter and a quoter. I could tote the bible and quote the bible with the best of them. Better than most! So why was it that I was just as miserable as when I was oblivious to anything about God's word and promises?

Remember the test I was telling you about, the one I was given at the Bradley Center? One of the questions was, "In the bible, what is the book of Genesis about?" Heck, I not only didn't know what it was about, I didn't even know where it was located. But now I was a walking theologian. People actually sought me out for "What I thought" about this scripture and that scripture. Imagine that! A born-again, baptized, bible toting, theologian, and still miserable as hell. I even taught a little Sunday school. Rejoice, rejoice in the lord, I would tell the class. The lord is your salvation and your deliverer. Had he delivered me? No!

The reminders! Everywhere I looked there were reminders. Her room was the same as it was the day the accident happened. I would go into her room, and the memories would come like a raging flood on the mighty Mississippi River overflowing and out of her banks. The trophies, hair ribbons, and stuffed animals, each one represented a moment in time. What's left after death? Nothing but memories.

When we first moved to Georgia we had a Z-28 with T tops. On sunny days Stephanie and I would ride around discovering new sights and places. The wind gusted through her long, black hair; her favorite CD blasted from the player. We were kings, queens, and princesses. The world was our kingdom. Now the kingdom was in ruins, wasted and laid barren by the one who "harvests from his fields."

I'm reminded of a song by the Eagles, "Take it Easy." "Don't let the wheels of your own mind drive you crazy." Those damn wheels, always spinning.

Something wasn't right. I was doing everything that I was supposed to do, receiving counseling, attending church, and moving on with my life. Or was I? Was this life? Daily visits to the cemetery, tending to a grave, removing every leaf that had blown on the sacred ground, empty evenings in an empty house, an empty marriage, and an empty heart. Yeah, those damn wheels will drive you crazy.

I went to counseling three times a week. A wonderful counselor, Miriam Kelly, listened to me and cried with me. July 14 was another one of those hot, humid days that are typical that time of year in Georgia. Today's counseling session had been extremely emotional and tiresome. I was putting every ounce of energy into my recovery, but there was no sunshine, just dark clouds rolling over me with my mood swings, laughing one moment, crying the next.

I was traveling toward home, the radio was on, but the volume was very low. I was talking to God. The same God who harvested from his field, the same God that I didn't even know if he existed. Talk to myself, Talk to my therapist, or talk to God? No need talking to myself; I didn't have the answers, and hey, I was a nut case and had papers to prove it. The therapist offered temporary comfort, but it lasted about as long as the ninety dollars an hour I was paying her. As for God, well, at least he didn't charge. Then again, he shouldn't. He had not delivered on any of his promises.

As I crossed over the square in LaGrange, a car shot out in front of me. I slammed on the brakes and extended my right arm over to the passenger side to protect Stephanie. She wasn't there. If you are a parent, you know the reflex motion of reaching over when you make a sudden stop to hold the passenger back. She wasn't there! Bastard! Learn how to drive.

As I continued along, something seemed to be telling me to turn up the radio. I tried ignoring that silent voice, but I felt compelled to turn up the radio. Playing was a song by Michael Bolton. Here is what I heard.

Gonna break these chains around me.
Gonna learn to fly again.
May be hard, may be hard,
But I'll do it
When I'm back on my feet again

Soon these tears will all be dryin'.
Soon these eyes will see the sun.
Might take time, might take time,
But I'll see it
When I'm back on my feet again.

When I'm back on my feet again
I'll walk proud down this street again
And they'll all look at me again
And they'll see that I'm strong.

Gonna hear the children laughing,
Gonna hear the voices sing,
Won't be long, won't be long
Till I hear them
When I'm back on my feet again.

Gonna feel the sweet light of heaven
Shining down its light on me

One sweet day, one sweet day.
I will feel it
When I'm back on my feet again.

When I'm back on my feet again
I'll walk proud down this street again
And they'll all look at me again
And they'll see that I'm strong.

And I'm not gonna crawl again.
I will learn to stand tall again.
No, I'm not gonna fall again
Cause I'll learn to be strong

When I'm back on my feet again.

Tears rushed forth, blocking my vision. I pulled to the side of the street, an emotional basket case crying uncontrollably. Would I be back on my feet again? How? How could I break the chains of death, dry the tears again, hear the children laughing again, the voices singing? Would I ever really stand tall again, be strong again? Sure I will! As soon as I am back on my feet again. Now, someone tell me, just how I do that?

Psalm 23:4 " Yea, though I walk through the valley of the shadow of death, I will feel no evil: for thou are with me; thy rod and thy staff comfort me."

I didn't walk through the valley of the shadow. I was the valley. I was in the deepest and darkest place possible. I didn't fear evil; I was evil.

I didn't realize it at that time, but I now know the incident with the car and song were no accident. Something, someone, was active inside of me, something or someone that had been present from the beginning. Since that day, May 8, 1990, I had been comforted by angels—Durwood and Anne Perry, Jeremy, Julia, Jason, Nikki Watts, Mariam Kelly, Larry and Ruth Ann, my loving wife who was pouring all of her energy into holding me together while herself traveling through the valley. Angels; I was surrounded by angels.

Was it possible I would be back on my feet again, Hear the laughter?

CHAPTER **11**

Hypocrisy and the Church

I HAD BECOME very involved in church. I was doing my best to be a born-again bible-toting Christian.

LaGrange, Georgia, is built around West Point Lake, 27,000 acres of fun and family recreation. Boating was a family activity for us. In the summer months we spent most weekends at the lake. By August the hot Georgia sun and drought conditions had taken their toll on the lake. Lake levels were low and the Army Corps of Engineers had issued a swimming advisory. Because of the lack of incoming water, there was an increase in bacteria in the lake. It was one of those deals where it probably wouldn't hurt you to swim in it, but to be safe, you probably shouldn't.

Sunday night, before church service started, we were gathered in small groups just making small talk. One of the deacons said, "Well, John, what do you think about the situation at the lake?" He knew that my family and I boated there. He said, "You know what the problem is, don't you?"

Of course I knew what the problem was. There wasn't enough rain. But he had another take on it. "It's all that Black (and he didn't use Black) piss, you know!"

I was stunned by his comment. "Pardon me," I said.

He said, "It's all that damn Black piss that Atlanta dumps into the river." I was shocked. This man was a deacon in the church and yet he used a belittling, racist word to refer to a group of people created by the God he served.

Race has never been an issue for me. White people, Blacks, Chinese, Russian, Mexican, were we not all God's people? And I would assume that the Whites in Atlanta pee also.

I remembered back to the time when Belinda and I had arrived home from the hospital after saying our goodbyes to Stephanie. My mother had met us in the driveway. "John, there's a Black (and she didn't use Black) woman in your house, and she is running the vacuum cleaner," she said. I had no idea what she was talking about. I went into the house and there was a woman, Eva Montgomery, who was under my supervision at work, and she was running the vacuum cleaner. I shut the vacuum off and asked, "Eva, what are you doing?"

She replied, "I just have to do something." Eva was Black. Was this the type of Black person that the good deacon spoke of? Maybe it was Al Simpson, a man, a Black man, who was also under my supervision. When I returned to work after Stephanie's death, Al had come into my office crying, telling me how sorry he was, and letting me know that if there was anything he could do for me, just let him know. He took my hand and prayed for me.

Was this the type of Black person the good deacon spoke about? How could this be? How can born-again Christians who proclaim to have received the spiritual rebirth have such a disdain for anything or any person God had created?

Two things had become apparent to me in my short time in the South. First, racial prejudice ran deep, and secondly, there was less love, compassion, and care in the church than one would expect from born-again believers.

If indeed there are places such as heaven and hell, a good many of these hallelujah, praise-the-lord, born-again, baptized brothers and sisters were destined to fuel the fires. And they think Georgia is hot!

Another instance that stands out concerns a phone call I received several months after the funeral. A local florist called and asked if I knew a certain person back in my home state. I didn't know the person personally, but the name was familiar, and I knew she was a friend of my mother's.

He said that the person had called the day before Stephanie's funeral and ordered flowers. The person was from out of state and didn't have a credit card, and the florist's usual business practice was not to accept orders from out of state without a credit card. He thought it unusual that the person hadn't placed the order through a local florist, but being as how it was the death of a child, he had agreed to take the order and bill the person for it. Several months had passed and his request for payment had gone unheeded.

I told him that I would contact my mother and tell her to remind her friend that payment was overdue. I called my mother, related the circumstances to her, and asked if she would touch base with the person.

My mother's reply was, "I can't do that; she is my friend."

I hung up the phone, and I ranted and raved. Her friend? What about her son? What about her granddaughter? The hell with her friend! The person was a deadbeat, and the reason the person had not placed the order locally was that the person's reputation for nonpayment preceded the person's presence. Damn that person! Damn my mother! Damn the world!

I was out of control. The doctor had given me a prescription for Xanax, the "chill pill." When things exploded, all I had to do was to take one. Well, if one is good, then unquestionably ten is better. Over the course of the next thirty minutes I took ten, but they had entirely no effect on me.

Belinda called the pastor, Durwood, and he and his wife, Ann, came to the house to help settle me down. They stayed with Belinda and me for the next five or six hours, talking and reasoning the best they could. Sometime in the wee hours of the morning the pills caught up with me, and I drifted off into sleep.

I continued to be active in the church. Sunday morning and evening, Wednesday evening, visitations, and even driving a van in the bus ministry. Yes, sir, I was a soldier in God's army. Onward Christian soldiers! To where? For what? I had no earthly idea.

There were many good and godly people in the church, but I was convinced that the greater part had really not seen the light. Was there a light? I didn't know.

Remember the story in the bible about Nicodemus? You know, the fellow who had come to Jesus in darkness asking what he must do? Jesus said, "You must be born again." I felt pretty sure that if some of the folks had been born again, the birth might have been different, but everything else, by all outwardly manifestation, was just a repeat of their life before the birth.

I had watched as one group of people led a charge to oust the youth pastor. They said it was because of funding, sort of like because there isn't any money, you got to go.

The youth pastor had done a remarkable job. In the several years that he had been there, the youth group had grown ten-fold.

Soon after we had moved to LaGrange, he and several of the youth had visited our home and invited Stephanie to be a part of their group. At that time I was troubled about her not attending church, and a group of friends had shown up to invite her to church. What a coincidence! Or was it?

Nevertheless, the youth pastor had to go. There wasn't any money. One of the deacons in the church and I sat down and reviewed the budget. We devised a proposal whereby we would have the funds to maintain the youth pastor's position. There were several ways to conserve. We were paying for a janitorial and lawn service. Those alone totaled one-half of the pastor's annual salary.

One Sunday night the matter was put before the congregation for a vote. The woman who was head of the finance committee gave a report and stated her and the finance committee's recommendation, for eliminating the position. She was heartbroken, she said, and she said she had "prayed and prayed about the matter."

The deacon and I both presented our findings and encouraged the members of the church to retain the position. The members voted, and the youth pastor's position was eliminated by a very slight margin.

After the meeting finished I was walking across the parking lot toward my car and I was approached by another deacon and a man whose wife was the church secretary.

The first word's out of the deacon's mouth were, "My kids don't like him, and he is not staying."

The other man joined in, "He is always giving my wife orders, telling her what to do." My god, it wasn't about money.

It was about little insecure people, born-again, baptized, church-going office holders who were so blinded with anger and hate that there was no way they could sing, "This little light of mine, I'm going to let it shine." The light, if there ever was any, had flickered and burnt out long ago.

Remember the woman who headed the finance committee, the one who had "prayed and prayed about the matter?" Several weeks later she walked away from her husband and two small children to be with the man with whom she had been having an affair. I still was not sure there was a God, but I was becoming rapidly convinced that there was indeed a devil, lots of them, and a good number of them were masquerading around as Christians.

I didn't want to be judgmental. The bible says not to judge, but if I am seeking the truth, how do I not judge? "If confusion is the first step to knowledge, I must be a genius." (Larry Leissner)

Not only am I a born-again Christian and a certified nut, now I am a genius. Still confused, but nevertheless a genius.

Despite the negatives in the church there are many positives In the church. Among the devils there many good and godly saints.

After Stephanie's accident people from the church started to show up at our house, some people I didn't even know, people like Walt Crane, Jasper Lumpkin, and John Hoff. Walt would show up each morning to make sure that the cooler was stocked with soft drinks and tea. So much food arrived that we had to ask them to give it to others; we had all that we needed.

Jasper had suffered the loss of his brother in an accident the same day that Stephanie died, but here was Jasper sitting with me, comforting me. His compassion for others was stronger than his own grief.

One day I was cleaning some fish I had caught, and John Hoff stopped by. He said, "Here, let me do that for you." I'm not sure if John was being compassionate or if he just wanted to get the knife out of my hand. I suspect it was passion.

CHAPTER 12

No Relief

NO RELIEF AT work, in the church, or at home. The only relief was when I visited my sanctuary, my own little sacred piece of ground.

Things hadn't gotten any better, nor had they gotten worse. Maybe life itself was creating a diversion from my thoughts of death. Each day was a blur. Busy, busy, busy! Always on the move, always on the run. I feared slowing down, in fear that I might catch up with myself. All I could cling to was the reflections of my life.

The greetings of people in trouble
Reflections of my life, oh, how they fill my eyes

All my sorrows, sad tomorrows
Take me back to my own home
All my cryings (all my cryings), feel I'm dying, dying
Take me back to my own home (oh I'm going home)

I'm changing, arranging, I'm changing
I'm changing everything, ah, everything around me

The world is a bad place, a bad place
A terrible place to live, oh, but I don't wanna die

All my sorrows, sad tomorrows
Take me back, to my old home
All my cryings, (all my cryings),feel I'm dying, dying
Take me back to my old home (I'm going home)

All my sorrows, sad tomorrows
Take me back, (take me back) to my old home
Sorrows, sad tomorrows, All my cryings (all my
cryings), feel I'm dying, dying! (Marmalade)

That's exactly how I felt. No changing, no arranging.

Damn the sorrows, damn the sadness, damn the crying, damn the world. The changing of sunlight to moonlight, reflections of my life, oh, how they fill my eyes, my mind, my heart.

Things were catching up with me again. A trip to the nut house, counseling, being born again, and the pain and suffering still hung over me like an old overcoat. Was there a God? I didn't know, and I was a born-again Christian, baptized, washed free of my sins, singing and shouting "Amen." I was doing everything by the blueprint. Yes, there is a blueprint for salvation. Ask any preacher. So where is this god that was to ease my heart and take away my pain and suffering?

I had to find relief. One Saturday morning I went to the liquor store and bought a fifth of liquor. If God couldn't or wouldn't take my pain away, maybe the answer was in a bottle.

I sat on my back porch and drank the whole fifth, yep the whole fifth, and got drunk as a skunk. Imagine that, a born-again Christian drunk as a skunk, and probably not the first one. The next morning I was sick, tired, and hung over. Not only was I sick, tired and hung over, but also that damn pain and hurt was still there. The answer was not to be found in a bottle.

As October approached the economy was slowing, and there were rumors that the company I worked for would be cutting back on middle- and upper-level management positions. Friday the twenty-ninth was the rumored dreaded "D" (discharge) date.

I'm going to have to start rolling the dice with the other hand. Snake eyes again! My position was one of the twelve eliminated.

That in itself wasn't that bad. During my career we had lived in five different states. Finding another position wouldn't be a problem. I felt sure that I could do it within a month.

But this time it was different. It wasn't that our roots weren't deeply entrenched in the area. The problem was that one of our branches was planted there. To load up and move across country was not an option. Time to check in and see what condition my condition was in. Let's see, marriage strained, no daughter, no job, and no desire.

Hey, no problem! I'll just go to church and shout, "Praise God, thank you, Jesus, I just want to thank you, Lord!" For what? I didn't know. Isn't that what Christians do?

Tell me about it, preacher. Tell me how I need to stand strong in the face of adversity, that my miracle is just around the corner. Tell me how God chastens those that he loves. And if you would, preacher, tell me how I am going to be able to pay my portion of the more than $200,000 in medical bills, burial expenses, house payments, and car payments while I also put food on the table.

And preacher, do me a favor. You apparently have a direct line to the top, so tell God not to love me so much. I'm not sure that I can take much more of this chastisement.

I would tell him myself, but there just seems to be this pattern of him not hearing me. He's probably tied up with prayers from adulterous committee members looking for ways to eliminate youth pastors with newborn babies. Yes, praise God, praise Jesus. That should help. Tomorrow the sun will shine brightly and there will be no more sorrows, sadness, or tears.

Sunday, May 8, 1991, Mother's Day: this was going to be tough one. The one-year anniversary of Stephanie's death. Do we go to church? How does a mother who has lost her child withstand a gathering that is honoring mothers and children?

We went. We were seated, and when I looked behind me, directly behind Belinda and me sat the young boy who was the object of all my anger and hate, the young boy who had brought the motor bike to our house. I could see Belinda's body trembling. Why in the world would God allow us to be put in this position?

The service began, the choir and congregation sang several hymns, the pastor shouted "Glory to God, what a wonderful day to be in God's house."

Really? Stand up, welcome someone, shake hands. Really?

I rose to my feet and was face-to- face with the young man. I could see the fear and apprehension in his face. At that moment the anger and hate toward him left my body. He meant no harm. He also was suffering. He had lost a friend, and his heart was torn.

I hugged the young man and told him that I loved him and that I would forgive him, but there was nothing to forgive him for. He was just as innocent in the horrible accident as Stephanie was. A calm settled over me, relief, not total relief, but the healing had begun.

CHAPTER **14**

The Devil's Sister

MONDAY MORNING, NO job to go to, nothing else to do, I might as well take a stroll to the mailbox. What is this? Internal Revenue Service, addressed to Mr. John I. Hart. You know what the IRS is all about? Money!

Now where was my faith? Here I was doubting, and all the good sisters and brothers who said they were going to pray for me had flooded the line with my prayer request, pushing aside the adulterous committee member, and my prayers had been answered. The government is always helping those in need. Granted, it is usually someone from another country that is the benefactor, but this time God had come through for a good ol' southern boy.

> Dear Mr. Hart:
>
> We have audited your return from 1987, and according to our calculations, you owe us $10,500." (Something like that.)
>
> Hot dog, I'm getting $10,500. Praise God. Thank you, Jesus!
>
> Wait a minute; I owe? How could I owe them anything? An accountant had done my taxes, and I have never held back anything. What is this government coming to? Accusing a born-again, baptized, church-going citizen of being fraudulent?

The reason stated was that I had taken a deduction for an early withdrawal that was available only to those over fifty-five years of age. It said to check line thirty-four. I did, and sure enough, I was guilty as charged.

Well, the accountant was the guilty one; after all, he had done the taxes. Would the IRS make him pay it? It was his mistake, not mine. No, not the one who prepares, but the payee, is responsible. Praise God, thank you, Jesus. This chastisement is killing me, smothering me. I can't take much more love.

I was still clinging to hope and what little faith I had, if any. The IRS had given me a date to appear in Atlanta. On the day I was to appear I prayed all the way. I said, "God, if you are real, you see the mess that I am in. I need your help. I can't do this alone. So please, please, help me."

I entered the Federal Building and went to the seventh floor. It reminded me of going into a bank. There were women lined up just like bank tellers. I stood in line and waited my turn. "Next," the woman yelled.

I approached the woman and showed her a copy of the letter I had received. I poured out my life story to her, the events of the past six months, and the dire straits I was in. I explained that it was a mistake and that I was willing to pay it, but I needed a little time, or maybe I could pay monthly.

With eyes as cold as a January morning in Vermont and a heart to match, she said I had two weeks to pay it or the IRS would attach all of my accounts and, if necessary, my property and sell it at public auction.

Thank you, Lord. Thank you. I asked, no, pleaded for help, and you sent me the devil's sister. So many times in the past six months when I needed help I went to the source, the well, only to find it dry.

On the drive back home, I thought, What a crock. If there was a God, he was not a God of mercy and grace, care, or compassion. Why should I continue? I'm a fixer. I'll fix this charade. I'll prove once and for all that there isn't a God. I saw a T-shirt that said Shit Just Happens! Ain't that the truth? Ain't that the truth?

Ruth Ann and I talked just about daily on the phone. Ruth and Larry were my rock, my anchor. I told her of my experience with the IRS. She and Larry offered to give us the money. I couldn't recall any time in my adult life that I had been in the position to ask for or accept anything.

I refused her offer. She insisted. She knew that my pride was standing in the way, and she didn't hesitate to tell me. I agreed to accept her offer, only as a loan, and that I be allowed to pay it back with interest, which I did six months later.

By then I was pretty well versed in the bible, and a scripture came to mind, *"Pride goeth before destruction, and a haughty spirit before a fall."* Exactly what did it mean? It dawned on me that I knew so many scriptures, yet I was questioning myself as to the meaning. Was there something deeper, beneath the scripture, beyond just the written word that I was failing to understand? Was the bible indeed the inspired word of God? Was there a god? So many question, and so few answers.

I figured I had one last effort left in me, one final decision to make. Turn to God or turn away from God. But before I could make that decision, I first had to determine if there was a god.

I started by studying the bible more. I purchased study guides and self-help books anywhere and everywhere that I could find them. Bible dictionaries, bibles galore, every version and edition lined my shelves. I would reference and cross reference, again and again. I needed to understand the meaning of every word and how the word applied to the scripture.

I stayed up until all hours of the morning, driven to find the fallacy in the infallible book. If it was there, I would find it, and then I would have peace. I could accept the fact that there wasn't a god much easier than I could accept the fact that he did exist and that he really couldn't care less about me or what happens in my life. Being alone during the day, I would boldly cry out and challenge God. "If you're there, reveal yourself. Answer me. You owe me an answer. Damn it, speak." Sometimes I would be so overcome with emotion that even in the shower I cried and banged on the walls. I would cry out, "Answer me. Tell me what I need to know. Prove that you exist!"

It had become a personal issue. Forget the church, the preacher, all the good sisters and brothers, or even the written word. It was now one-on-one, me against God, the flesh against the spirit. I've heard people of prayer speak about, rattling the gates of hell. I don't know about that, but if there was indeed a heaven, I was shaking the foundation. I was following the yellow brick road, off to see the wizard. I wasn't seeking a brain, a heart, or even courage. I wanted answers, and I wanted them now.

The more noise I made, the more silence I received, not even a peep from the great almighty. It was an obsession. My mother told me that I was going to drive myself crazy. My uncle said to "quit reading all those self-help books." My aunt told me to pray.

My mind told me to push on, to demand, to pursue answers.

CHAPTER 15

The Revealing

WHAT WAS BEHIND all of the madness? If there was a god, then there had to be a heaven and a hell. If so, where was my baby? Had I failed? Was my daughter paying for the sins of her father? Oh God, no, please, God, take me. I'm responsible. I failed, not her. Take my soul and burn it for eternity, but not my baby, please, God, not my baby!

The question was one I was afraid to ask, a topic I dared not discuss with anyone else. I wanted to know the answer. Or did I? I studied the theology of various denominations of Christian faiths. Once saved, always saved? That's what the Baptists said. Not true, said some of those of the Pentecostal and Holiness faith. Age of accountability? No one had an answer for that one. Eight years, two years, thirteen years? Did it have anything to do with age? Was it based on maturity? What about those who had never heard the word at all? What about the mentally impaired?

It was sorta like knocking over the milk jugs at the county fair. Knock them all over and win the prize of your choice. Which one do I choose? The one that gives me the greatest comfort? Never any answers, just one question leading to another question. What is this thing called salvation? How is one saved?

Believe? Believe and be baptized? Is the salvation in the belief or in the baptizing? Wait, some say that is not enough. A true Christian bears fruit. So believe, be baptized, throw in some works?

Still not enough? How about believe, be baptized, works, and speak in tongues? Does that get the job done? In my home state there are some who say you have to take up serpents. Do what? If my salvation depends on me taking up a serpent, then fire up the furnace; I'm hell bound.

I have nothing but the utmost respect for those who demonstrate their faith by taking up a serpent, but my fear of snakes is greater than my fear of not knowing.

A little about speaking in tongues: as a Baptist, some say there is no such thing, that speaking in tongues is not necessary now; it passed away. Some Baptists say that they believe in speaking in tongues, but they don't practice it. Which is it? I believe it is something that people have to work out with themselves and with God. I know what I know, and here is what I know.

One day I was deep in prayer and meditation, still asking, still seeking, still knocking. The power of God came upon me. Yep, God's Holy Spirit paid me a visit. My body tingled, and it seemed as if my spirit left my body and was floating above me. A fog, a mist surrounded me.

Details? I can't give you a lot of detail, but I can tell you what I know. I know that I was pacing back and forth from one end of the house to the other, crying, tears flowing, hands raised. I was talking, maybe preaching, maybe praising, I'm not sure.

About an hour later my spirit returned to my body and I was standing in the family room. My body was drenched. A calm and peace settled about me that I had never experienced before and have not I since. The Spirit of God had visited this born-again Christian and left a mark, an assurance, that there is a much higher power, a power that is within me, a reserve that can be called upon in my time of struggles and fears.

Why so much confusion? Can they all be right? Can they all be wrong? The wheels of my own mind were driving me crazy with sorrows, crying, and asking if the world is a bad place, a terrible place to live. Reflections of my life, oh, how they fill my eyes.

All my sorrows, sad tomorrows
Take me back to my own home

That's all I wanted, just to be taken back to my own home, a place in time when my life was full, when laughter and joy filled the rooms. I could hear the children laugh again.

Gonna feel the sweet light of heaven
Shining down its light on me
One sweet day, one sweet day
I will feel it
When I'm back on my feet again.

One sweet day, when I can wrap my arms around Stephanie, smell her fragrance, and see her smile. Yes, that's when I will be back on my feet again. Just roll back the hands of time. Take me back to my own home, the home I had before May 8, 1990.

CHAPTER 17

God Speaks

THE BATTLE CONTINUED. Day and night, I had more questions, demands for answers, but received nothing but silence. Exhausted, mentally and physically, I was too tired to fight, too devastated to quit. One night I fell into a deep sleep. Something was happening, something strange. I could feel and see my body floating upward, higher and higher, floating in space above an ancient city. I know that there are some who will say that I was hallucinating or dreaming. Some might even say that I had fallen completely over the edge, but I know what I know.

I was above the city. I could see the domes and rooftops, see the smoke from the chimneys. A voice spoke to me. No, it wasn't like thunder; actually it wasn't even a voice. It was more like a thought that was being conveyed to me. "Do you want to see her face?" I replied, "Yes." I looked to my right, and there was Stephanie. My baby, oh, my baby. She had a peace about her, and happiness seemed to emit from her very presence. She did not speak to me nor I to her. The joy that filled my heart is indescribable. My baby, my precious baby.

The voice spoke again, or conveyed the thought, "She is okay. It is not your time yet, but soon." I was wide awake, lying in bed, shocked, terrified, or amazed? I'm not sure.

Was I dreaming, fantasizing, hallucinating? I was filled with joy but at the same time gripped with fear. " It is not your time yet, but soon." What did that mean?

I called my aunt the next day and shared the experience with her. I was dying! It was not my time yet, but soon. For a year I had relentlessly pursued the truth. Banged on the doors to heaven and rattled the gates of hell. I had been persistent, downright determined to discover the truth, and I had.

There was a God, my baby was in heaven, and my life on this earth was drawing to a close.

Seemed like a Pyrrhic victory to me. A Pyrrhic victory is one with devastating cost to the victor. The phrase is an allusion to King Pyrrhus of Epirus, whose army suffered irreplaceable casualties in defeating the Romans at Heraclea in 280 BC and Asclum in 279 BC during the Pyrrhic War. After the latter battle, Plutarch relates the following in a report by Dionysius:

"The armies separated; and, it is said, Pyrrhus replied to one that gave him joy of his victory that one more such victory would utterly undo him. For he had lost a great part of the forces he brought with him, and almost all his particular friends and principal commanders; there were no others there to make recruits, and he found the confederates in Italy backward. On the other hand, as from a fountain continually flowing out of the city, the Roman camp was quickly and plentifully filled up with fresh men, not at all abating in courage for the loss they sustained, but even from their very anger gaining new force and resolution to go on with the war."

In both of Pyrrhus's victories, the Romans lost more men than Pyrrhus did; however, the Romans had a much larger supply of men from which to draw soldiers, so their losses did less damage to their war effort than Pyrrhus's losses did to his.

Had the cost to the victor been devastating? In the beginning I had set out to prove the nonexistence of God and along the way had stumbled upon the reality that there is indeed a God. Next, questioning the fate of my child, I arrived at peace, at least with that issue. Doubt meets deity; deity conquers.

Every time there was an answer, there was another question. What about me? What about my relationship, my commitment to serving God? Am I even saved? Sure, I believed, if not before, believe me, I had moved beyond believing to knowing. I had been baptized. Was that enough?

Repenting? Well, it seemed that for me it was a daily thing. I really was trying. The more I studied scripture, the longer the list requiring repentance became. Do this, don't do that, practice this, don't practice that, read this, watch that, don't read that, don't watch this.

Signs, Signs, everywhere a sign
Blocking out the scenery breaking my mind
Do this, don't do that, can't you read the sign

I couldn't read the signs. I couldn't even get a grasp on those giving the signals. Back to the question that Nicodemus ask of Jesus. "What must I do to be saved?" Jesus replied, "You must be born again." This I understood. What I didn't understand was the method of birthing.

Back to the theology. Who is right? Who is wrong? I am a Baptist. Why? Because that was the church that Stephanie chose, because her friends went there.

Are Baptists saved? Immersion or sprinkling? Do women wear their hair in a bun or let it grow to the floor? Makeup or natural? Speak in tongues or take up a serpent? What must I do to be saved?

It appeared to me that there were as many different versions of the birthing method as there were those willing to expound it. One book, but so many versions, saved one moment, lost the next. How can that be? I thought it was once saved, always saved.

Here I go again. Back to the bible, back to the questions, forward to the future. What must I do to be saved?

I began my quest for the truth about salvation as I do most things, full steam ahead. My focus was on the New Testament.

"The same came to Jesus by night, and said unto him, Rabbi, we know that thou art a teacher come from God: for no man can do these miracles that thou doest, except God be with him. Jesus answered and said unto him, Verily, verily, I say unto thee, Except a man be born again, he cannot see the kingdom of God. Nicodemus saith unto him, How can a man be born when he is old? can he enter the second time into his mother's womb, and be born? Jesus answered, Verily, verily, I say unto thee, Except a man be born of water and of the Spirit, he cannot enter into the kingdom of God. That which is born of the flesh is flesh; and that which is born of the Spirit is spirit. Marvel not that I said unto thee, Ye must be born again." John 3:1-7

Jesus answered; that was good enough for me. If the Son of God had given the answer, it would stand the test of time. What is the mystery of the new birth? Is there a mystery? No, there wasn't any mystery. Ask ten preachers, and you'll get ten slightly different variations of the new birth.

To understand this biblical term, it is necessary to understand that there are two births. The "first" birth is the physical birth, when you were born into this world from your mother and father. When the bible speaks of being "born of water," it is speaking about the physical birth, not baptism. The "second birth" is a spiritual birth, which means to be born of the spirit, God's Holy Spirit.

This raises a couple of questions. Why does a person need to be born spiritually? And what is a "spiritual" birth? The bible teaches that man is created in the image of God. God manifests Himself to mankind in the persons of God the Father, God the Son, and God the Holy Spirit. Likewise, mankind is composed of a body, soul, and spirit.

Our body is the tent, you could say, of the soul and spirit; the body is a temporary dwelling place. Our soul is composed of the heart (to feel), the mind (to think), and the will (to decide). Our spirit is dead in sin when we are born; that is, we are born void of God. No person is ever born with God. The only exception is the Lord Jesus

Christ, who came as God in the flesh

(1st Timothy 3:16). *Our spirit is dead in trespasses and sin the Bible says.*

"And you hath he quickened, who were dead in trespasses and sins; Wherein in time past ye walked according to the course of this world, according to the prince of the power of the air, the spirit that now worketh in the children of disobedience:" Ephesians 2:1,2

The unsaved person cannot understand God.

"But the natural man receiveth not the things of the Spirit of God: for they are foolishness unto him: neither can he know them, because they are spiritually discerned." 1st Corinthians 2:14

Now, let me get this straight. The unsaved person cannot understand God, but to be saved one must understand God's word? That thought creates a dilemma doesn't it?

Read, research, study, and pray. That was pretty much my life 24/7. The more I put into it, the more God poured out his revelations. If my salvation is based on belief, baptism, obedience, or church membership, can it really be eternal?

None of these things are eternal. Belief can change; water will pass away; total obedience is impossible; I might stop going to church. Would someone please tell me what secures my salvation?

The blood; nothing but the blood. When the Lord Jesus Christ shed his holy blood as the atonement for my sins, salvation was secured; the final act, the covenant sealed.

CHAPTER 18

Again He Speaks

ONCE AGAIN I had an encounter with God. God came to me in the middle of night when I was in a dead sleep. I could see a bright, beautiful blue sky. There appeared a small dot in the sky and the blue sky and clouds were sucked into the dot like a whirlwind, leaving only black. Then the whirlwind reversed and the darkness was replaced by the blue sky and clouds.

God spoke to me saying, "You have what you need." He had shown me that my life had been filled with beauty and brightness, and then the beauty and brightness had been filled with darkness, but the beauty and brightness would return.

"Quit worrying about what you need and what you have. You have what you need, and I will supply what you don't have. Will you receive it?"

Matthew 7:7 *Ask, and it shall be given you; seek, and ye shall find; knock, and it shall be opened unto you.*

Again a deep sleep. I awoke to see an angel at the foot of my bed. She was dressed in white and surrounded by a gold glow, and she was transparent. I could see right through her. The angel was floating at the foot of the bed, her arms opening and closing, motioning toward the wall. I looked at the wall where several family photos were hanging on the wall.

At that time Belinda and I were sleeping in different rooms, and I called out to her to come. I asked if she saw that, and she replied, "See what?"

"The angel, the angel floating at the foot of the bed."

She replied, "John, I don't see anything."

"Surely you see it. How can you not see it?"

The angel floated across the room and disappeared into the wall where family photos were hanging. What was the meaning of the angel? I'm still not sure. I do believe that it had something to do with family. Was the angel saying that someday we would be a family again? When I look back on it I can just imagine the morning conversations between God and Jesus.

Jesus: "Is he back again?"
God: "He never left."
Jesus: "He's determined, isn't he?"
God: "The boy never gives up."
Jesus: "He will make a good one."

Now you might be thinking, yep, John is a nut case. He claims that God spoke to him and is speaking to him. I'm okay with that. People can think what they want to think. I know what I know. Why me? Why would God speak to me? Maybe because I never quit asking, never quit seeking, never quit knocking.

The answers I sought could not be found in the church, in fellowship, in baptism, singing, shouting, or praising. I thank God for these things, but my beef wasn't with the church; it was with God. The only acceptable answers had to come from God and God only.

Have you ever given any thought as to what prayer is? Ask ten people, and again you will get ten different answers. Prayer is communicating.

When I was angry at God, crying out to God, cursing God, demanding answers, I thought I was venting, but I was actually praying, communicating. I personally wouldn't recommend that method, but if all else fails, let it fly. Ask, seek, knock. God has broad shoulders, and God wants to hear from us, communicate with us, fellowship with us.

Jesus: "How is he today?"
God: "He's on the warpath again."
Jesus: "Do you think he will give up?"
God: "Not this one. He's in for the long haul."

If you get only one thing out of these writings, let it be never give up, never become complacent. If we are to grow spiritually, we must continue to ask, seek, and knock.

CHAPTER 19

It's Not Your Time Yet, but Soon

I WAS SECURE in my belief and faith, and the years continued. I continued to grow stronger spiritually. My wife, my son, and my grandkids have all been saved by the Grace of God. The work is done, my journey complete, and I can now kick back and enjoy the peace and security that God had given me. Well, nope, not yet.

On May 15, 2004, I was ordained into the ministry by Teaver Road Baptist Church. Fourteen years to the day after we had buried Stephanie. Imagine that. A journey of fourteen years led me from the pit to the pulpit; destruction became divinity.

God impressed upon my heart that I was to preach. Whoa! Put the brakes on. I didn't ask for that.

> **God:** "No, you didn't, but that is what I have chosen for you."
> **Me:** "I don't want to be a preacher."
> **God:** "Why not?"
> **Me:** "I don't have the personality of a preacher."
> **God:** "What is wrong with your personality?"
> **Me:** "Nothing. I like my personality."
> **God:** "So do I. You will do just fine."
> **Me:** "I'm not slicking my hair back and looking like a mortician."
> **God:** "Didn't ask you to."
> **Me** "I am too blunt and straight to the point."
> **God:** "Exactly. The church needs more of that."

One of my favorite books is *The Autobiography of Peter Cartright.* Cartright, also known as The Kentucky Boy, was a traveling Methodist revivalist. He was a circuit rider. Circuit rider clergy, in the earliest years of the United States, were clergy assigned to travel around specific geographic territories to minister to settlers and organize congregations.

When a Methodist or Baptist preacher felt that God had called him to preach, instead of hunting up a college or biblical institute, hunted up a hardy pony and some traveling apparatus, and with his library always at hand, namely a bible, hymn book, and Methodist or Baptist discipline, he started. With a text that never wore out or grew stale, he cried, *"Behold the Lamb of God that taketh away the sin of the world."*

I didn't want to deal with the daily inner workings of a local congregation. I wanted nothing to do with the business dealings, the politics, the dirty deacons, or the secretaries gone astray. I wanted to cry out, *"Behold the Lamb of God that taketh away the sin of the world."*

Reverend John Hart

The Circuit Rider Ministries was established and with my hardy pony (car) traveling apparatus (clothes), and a bible I set out to share God's Holy Word. I have been privileged to share in most denominations and have been blessed and hope those hearing the Word were blessed.

I never intended to write a book. I was writing my inner feelings as part of therapy in my attempt to just survive, feelings that I had not shared with anyone in thirty years. God has impressed upon me to share my experience with the world and *Stephanie's Story, Not My Time Yet* , came to life.

Some people have asked about the title. I don't believe that the journey I have taken would have happened without Stephanie's life and death. I do believe that her spirit has traveled with me as I journeyed.

If you have purchased and read *Stephanie's Story*, it is because you or someone you know needs to know that there is hope, that you can experience a full life even after a devastating loss.

When I was a teenager, a childhood friend was killed in a car wreck. He lived across the street from me and was like the big brother I never had. His house was full of life, joy, and happiness. His father planted a large garden, and his mother was always tending to her flowers. When my friend died, for all practical purposes his mother and father died.

There were no more gardens or flowers and the sun that had shown brightly over the house was no longer visible. Their lives and their home were gloom and doom, and I never saw them smile again. The life had been sucked out of their body. It doesn't have to be that way.

CHAPTER 20

The Anchor Holds

I CAN'T TELL you that my life or me as a person are perfect. I can't say that my spiritual growth has restored me to the place in life I was before May 8, 1990. There is not a day that goes by that I do not miss Stephanie. Her picture is the screen saver on my phone. I can, however, tell you that I am back on my feet again and I can hear the birds sing again. I can tell you that being a Christian, a person of faith, does not shield me from the evils and misfortunes of life. I can tell you that God's Grace and Mercy have lifted me above my circumstances. I can tell you that the reflections of my life no longer fill my eyes with tears. Praise God; the anchor still holds.

God has blessed me with three wonderful grandchildren, two who have been actively involved in my life. I have watched them grow into spiritual, mature young people who have helped me break the chains, fly again, and hear the laughter and the singing. I give thanks to God for allowing me to be part of Johnathon's, Barbara's, and Belinda Grace's life. Pa loves you.

I can't tell you that God's church is perfect. It isn't. The church is filled with good godly people and the church is filled with imperfect people, people battling their own demons, people who are walking through a dark valley. I can tell you that I could not have survived without God's church, God's Word, and God's people.

I can tell you that I don't think it is humanly possible for anyone to go deeper into that dark valley than I did. I can tell you that God guided me and lifted me from that valley. I can tell you that God is wanting, willing, and able to do the same for you.

I can tell you that God and the church are my refuge, my strength, my faith, my hope, that God loves me, and He loves you. In our most difficult times, times when we feel He has abandoned us, He is present. Seek and we shall find. Never quit seeking.

I can tell you not to give up. Knock, and the door shall be opened. Keep on knocking. Never quit knocking. If knocking isn't working, start kicking. God has broad shoulders, and He can withstand your attack.

The past thirty years have gone by fast. As I approach my seventieth year of age and look back, I can best sum up my life as normal and natural. Many people have, are, or will be going through a dark valley, some because of a death, some because of divorce, some because of financial difficulties, and some because of depression. Although the circumstances can be different, the journey is the same. We do not have to travel the road alone.

One day I will cross the river Jordan into the promise land. I'll fall at the feet of my Lord and Savior, giving honor and glory. With loving hands he will lift me up and say, "I know the desires of your heart. She is over there." Once again, forever and ever, all eternity, she will be daddy's girl.

Never quit asking. Ask for God's forgiveness, His love, His guidance, His Spirit to flood your soul. We have not because we ask not. Ask!

Blessed be the God and Father of our Lord Jesus Christ, the Father of mercies and God of all comfort, who comforts us in all our affliction, so that we may be able to comfort those who are in any affliction, with the comfort with which we ourselves are comforted by God. (2 Corinthians 1:3-4)

May God Comfort and Bless you.

It might not be your time yet, but soon.